Quiz: 116055

Level: 6.2

Points: 1.0

The Lewis and Clark Expedition

The Lewis and Clark Expedition

Judith Bloom Fradin &
Dennis Brindell Fradin

LEWIS AND CLARK EXPEDITION
1804 1954
UNITED STATES POSTAGE 3¢

mc Marshall Cavendish
Benchmark

New York

Dedication

For our grandson, Aaron Bernard Todd Fradin, with love

Acknowledgments

The authors thank Butch "Mr. Keelboat" Bouvier of Onawa, Iowa, for his help

Marshall Cavendish Benchmark
99 White Plains Road
Tarrytown, NY 10591
www.marshallcavendish.us

Library of Congress Cataloging-in-Publication Data
Fradin, Judith Bloom.
The Lewis and Clark Expedition / by Judith Bloom Fradin & Dennis Brindell Fradin.
p. cm. — (Turning points in U.S. history)
Includes bibliographical references and index.
ISBN-13: 978-0-7614-2044-6
1. Lewis and Clark Expedition (1804–1806)—Juvenile literature. 2. West (U.S.)—Discovery and exploration—Juvenile literature.
3. West (U.S.)—Description and travel—Juvenile literature. I. Fradin, Dennis B.
II. Title. III. Series.
F592.7.F73 2007
917.804'2—dc22
2006031536

Photo research by Connie Gardner

Cover photo: A detail of a sculpture of Lewis and Clark by Stanley Wanlass, located in Oregon
Title Page: A 1954 U.S. postage stamp commemorates the Expedition's 150th anniversary

Cover photo: Connie Ricca/CORBIS
Title page: *The Granger Collection:*
The photographs in this book are used by permission and through the courtesy of: *The Granger Collection:* 16, 34; *Corbis:* Bettmann, 6, 12, 17, 42-43;
Connie Ricca, 18, 30, 32; Tom Bean, 20; *NorthWind Picture Archives:* 8, 9, 10, 15, 23, 25, 26, 36; *Getty Images:* Aurora, 28.

Time Line: *Corbis:* Bettmann

Editor: Deborah Grahame
Publisher: Michelle Bisson
Art Director: Anahid Hamparian

Printed in Malaysia
1 3 5 6 4 2

Contents

CHAPTER ONE: "Across This Continent"   7

CHAPTER TWO: "We Set Out in High Spirits"   13

CHAPTER THREE: "These Are My People!"   21

CHAPTER FOUR: "Ocian in View! O! the Joy!"   29

CHAPTER FIVE: The Voyagers Return   33

CHAPTER SIX: "All the Success Which Could Have Been Expected"   37

Glossary   40

Timeline   42

Further Information   44

Bibliography   46

Index   47

This painting depicts the transfer of land from a representative of France to a U.S. Commissioner in the Louisiana Purchase of 1803.

CHAPTER ONE

"Across This Continent"

The United States was born on July 4, 1776, when American leaders issued the **Declaration of Independence**. At first the nation consisted of just thirteen states along the east coast.

As Americans moved westward, new states were formed. Vermont, Kentucky, Tennessee, and Ohio had joined the Union by 1803. That year the United States acquired a huge new territory. For $15 million (equivalent to about $300 million today), the United States bought 828,000 square miles of land (2,144,000 square kilometers) west of the Mississippi River from France. This **Louisiana Purchase** doubled the size of the United States.

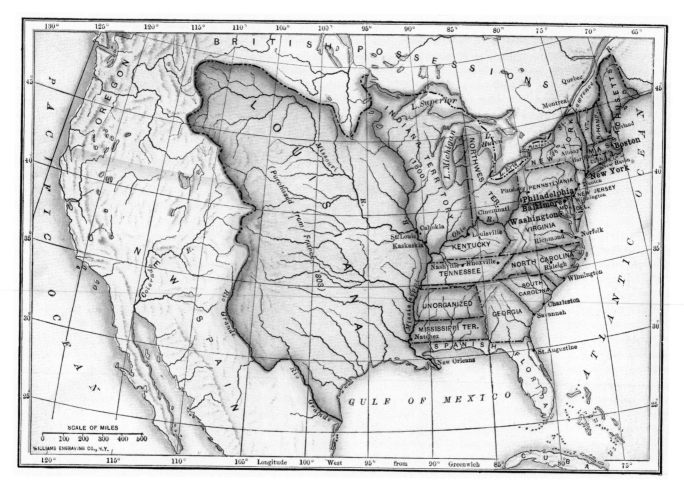

This map shows the large area of land that the United States gained as a result of the Louisiana Purchase.

Little was known about the western territory obtained in the Louisiana Purchase. What kind of land and climate did it have? What people, animals, and plants lived there?

Meriwether Lewis

Meriwether Lewis was born on a plantation in Virginia's Albemarle County. Meriwether was a curious child who loved the outdoors.

Lewis became a soldier and served for a time in a company of sharpshooters led by William Clark. Later, he was the personal aide to President Jefferson, who chose him to lead the Corps of Discovery. Despite the hardships, the long journey was the highlight of Lewis's life.

After the expedition, President Jefferson appointed him governor of the Louisiana Territory. Lewis later had personal problems that lead him to take his own life at age thirty-five.

Meriwether Lewis (1774–1809)

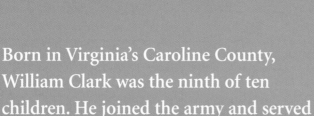

William Clark

Born in Virginia's Caroline County, William Clark was the ninth of ten children. He joined the army and served in several campaigns.

In 1803 Clark received a letter from Meriwether Lewis, inviting him to serve as the Corps of Discovery's cocaptain. The tall, red-headed Clark wrote accounts of events that occurred during the journey. He was also the expedition's chief mapmaker. One thing he *could not* do very well was spell. For example, he described how Indians provided the travelers with tasty "Water Millions." Of course, he meant "watermelons." After the expedition, Clark served as governor of the Missouri Territory. He died at age sixty-eight.

William Clark (1770–1838)

President Thomas Jefferson decided to send out an **expedition** to explore parts of the Louisiana Purchase region. The explorers would also travel through what are now Idaho, Washington, and Oregon— the Pacific Northwest—all the way to the Pacific Ocean. This would strengthen U.S. claims to the Pacific Northwest region, which Great Britain also wanted.

President Jefferson asked his personal secretary, Meriwether Lewis, to lead the expedition "across this continent." Lewis agreed, but insisted that his old army friend, William Clark, serve as his cocaptain. For their crew, Captains Lewis and Clark assembled a team of forty-three rugged men who could hunt, handle horses, and build boats and forts. The team included Clark's slave, an African-American man named York. Also making the trip would be Captain Lewis's big dog, a Newfoundland named Seaman.

The Corps of Discovery traveled upriver using special rowboats with sails.

CHAPTER TWO

"We Set Out in High Spirits"

The Lewis and Clark Expedition, also known as the **Corps of Discovery**, set out from the St. Louis, Missouri, area on May 14, 1804. Thanks to journals kept by Lewis, Clark, and several of their men, a great deal is known about their journey. "We Set out in high Spirits for the western Expedition," Virginia-born Joseph Whitehouse wrote in his journal.

They began by heading up the Missouri River in a **barge** and two **pirogues**. Traveling roughly 10 miles (16 km) a day, the men proceeded upriver. Generally they rowed their boats, but sometimes when the wind was right they used sails. In places where there were **rapids**, the men got out of the boats and walked along the shore, using ropes to pull the vessels upstream. At times Lewis, Clark, and some of the men ventured beyond the riverbanks to explore or hunt.

Each day brought new challenges. They were caught in violent storms. On the tenth day of the journey, Lewis fell off a cliff. He "saved himself," Clark reported, by plunging his knife into the cliffside to break his fall. Joseph Field survived a snake bite. Charles Floyd was not as lucky. On August 20, 1804, Floyd died, perhaps from a ruptured appendix. He was buried on a bluff in present-day Sioux City, Iowa. The youngest member of the Corps, nineteen-year-old George Shannon, got lost while out hunting and could not find the expedition for more than two weeks.

By late October 1804, the explorers had reached what is now central North Dakota, where they decided to spend the winter. They had covered 1,500 miles (2,400 km) in their first five months of travel. Near several Indian villages, they built a cluster of cabins which they called Fort Mandan.

The winter of 1804–05 was very difficult for the explorers. At times the temperature at Fort Mandan dipped to as low as –20, –40, and even –45 degrees Fahrenheit. The expedition's hunters sometimes came back empty-handed, but Mandan Indians from nearby villages supplied the explorers with corn. And a key addition to the Corps of Discovery was made at Fort Mandan.

Lewis and Clark knew that, later in their journey, they would need

This footpath runs through a prairie on Lewis and Clark's route near Mandan, North Dakota.

horses to cross the mountains. They hoped to obtain these horses from the Shoshone Indians. But how would they communicate with the Shoshone when they met them?

A young Shoshone woman named Sacagawea lived near Fort Mandan. Some five years earlier, she had been kidnapped by Minnetaree Indians who had raided her people's village in Montana.

Sacagawea

The young Shoshone woman who accompanied Lewis and Clark was born in present-day Idaho in 1789 or 1790. She was given the name Sacagawea, meaning "Bird Woman," perhaps because she was small and graceful like a bird.

Sacagawea was happy to join the Corps of Discovery, for it meant that she might be reunited with her family and friends out West. And no one did more for the expedition than she did. She found food, rescued supplies, and helped obtain horses, while traveling thousands of miles with a baby on her back. Sadly, Sacagawea lived only a few years after the expedition. She died at a trading post in what is now South Dakota after giving birth to her daughter, Lisette, in late 1812, at age twenty-two or twenty-three. William Clark, who had adopted Pomp earlier, also adopted Lisette after Sacagawea's death.

A bronze sculpture of Sacagawea and Pomp stands in Salmon, Idaho.

As an interpreter, Sacagawea was a key member of the Lewis and Clark Expedition.

The Minnetaree had brought Sacagawea to North Dakota, where Toussaint Charbonneau, a French-Canadian fur trader from Canada, took her for his wife. The fur trader and the young Shoshone woman settled in one of the Indian villages near Fort Mandan.

York

Born in Virginia around 1770, York was a slave belonging to the Clark family. He became William Clark's personal slave when they were both about fourteen years old. He had to help his master dress, serve him his meals, and do whatever else William Clark ordered.

York is examined by curious Native Americans.

York was a valuable member of the expedition. As a skilled hunter, he supplied elk, bison, and ducks for the Corps to eat. He cared for Charles Floyd when he became very ill. He also fascinated the Indians. Never having seen a black person before, some of them apparently believed that York's skin was *painted* black.

At the end of the journey, the other expedition members were paid in money and land, but York and Sacagawea received nothing. Clark finally freed York around 1816. York returned to Kentucky and worked in the area hauling goods by wagon. York died sometime before 1832.

Charbonneau heard that Lewis and Clark needed someone who could speak and **translate** the Shoshone language. He brought Sacagawea, who was pregnant, to meet Lewis and Clark. Sacagawea could speak Shoshone because she *was* a Shoshone, Charbonneau explained. He, too, could be of help because he knew the French and Minnetaree languages, the fur trader added. Lewis and Clark agreed to pay Charbonneau $500 if he and Sacagawea would join the expedition.

Now part of the Corps of Discovery, Sacagawea and Charbonneau moved into Fort Mandan. They shared a cabin with Lewis, Clark, and York. On February 11, 1805, Sacagawea, who was only about fifteen years old, gave birth to a baby boy at the fort. Charbonneau gave his son a French name—Jean Baptiste. The members of the expedition called the child Pomp.

Lewis and Clark hoped that, despite bringing a baby along, Sacagawea would be of help when they resumed their journey. They could not have known just how helpful she would be.

This replica, or exact copy, of Fort Mandan was built in 1972 near the site of the original structure.

CHAPTER THREE

"These Are My People!"

In April, Lewis and Clark sent several men and the barge loaded with **specimens** back east to President Jefferson. The souvenirs for the president included a live prairie dog, four live magpies, many plants, and an Indian buffalo robe. On April 7, 1805, the thirty-three members of the Corps of Discovery—now including Sacagawea, Charbonneau, and their eight-week-old son, Pomp—set out from Fort Mandan. Their boat builders had been busy over the winter. They were now traveling in six small canoes and the two pirogues.

Sacagawea was an enormous help from the start. On the third day out of Fort Mandan, she found some tasty roots while walking along the shore, and cooked them for dinner. Later in the journey, Sacagawea would find wild licorice, currants, gooseberries, and wild onions. These foods provided a welcome relief from the travelers' usual meals of corn-meal and dry meat.

One foggy day, Sacagawea prevented a major disaster. On May 14, 1805, Lewis and Clark were walking along the Missouri River shore. Sacagawea, with Pomp on her back, was in one of the pirogues, along with Charbonneau and several other men. Three hundred feet from shore, the pirogue was suddenly struck by a strong wind gust. As the boat tipped over and filled with water, Charbonneau yelled that he could not swim. Knowing that she could swim to shore with Pomp on her back if she had to, Sacagawea calmly grabbed the supplies that were floating away, while the men bailed out the boat. Captain Clark reported in his journal:

The articles which floated out was nearly all caught by [Sacagawea]. In this pirogue were our papers, instruments, books, medicine, and almost every article necessary to insure the success of the enterprize.

Had these precious supplies been lost, the voyagers might have been forced to turn back. To thank Sacagawea, Lewis and Clark later named a stream in central Montana after her.

In his journal, William Clark recorded daily events of the journey. He provided detailed drawings of plants and animals he observed, as well.

There were many other hardships on the westward journey. The mosquitoes were sometimes so thick that they made Seaman howl at night and turned the travelers' bodies into masses of red sores. There were close calls with rattlesnakes. One Corps member after another became ill with flu, severe diarrhea, and fevers. Sacagawea was ill most of the month of June, and she nearly died.

No matter how bad they felt, the travelers continued their journey. In June 1805 they came to the Great Falls of the Missouri River in Montana. They had to transport their boats around these waterfalls by land. This process is called **portaging**. Placing the boats on wheels made from slices of a tree trunk, they pushed and pulled the vessels across the land. Cactus thorns pierced their **moccasins** and entered their feet. Grizzly bears approached their camp at night and were scared away by Seaman. The travelers endured rainstorms, flash floods, and hail so intense that it bounced 10 feet (3 meters) high after hitting the ground.

In early July the portage was completed and the Corps of Discovery continued up the Missouri River in their vessels. On July 22 the expedition reached a creek that Sacagawea recognized. Soon after, she showed the men the spot where the Minnetaree had kidnapped her. But as days passed and no Shoshone appeared, Lewis and Clark grew desperate. How would they cross the mountains without Shoshone horses?

The explorers went searching for Sacagawea's people. On August 13 Captain Lewis and a small party of men arrived at a Shoshone camp in what is now Idaho. Using **sign language**, Lewis convinced the chief of this Shoshone band to come meet the other members of the Corps of Discovery. The chief agreed, but dozens of warriors accompanying him feared that Lewis was leading them into a trap.

When a large party of strangers carrying guns came into view, the Shoshone became so panicky that a battle seemed likely. The Shoshone warriors were reaching for their bows when they saw something that calmed their fears.

A young Indian woman with a baby on her back was with the intruders. Suddenly, she began dancing and sucking on her fingers—a

A buffalo is standing on a cliff overlooking the Great Falls of the Missouri River in Montana.

Shoshone sign meaning "These are my people!" Seeing Sacagawea's gestures, the Indians realized that the white men's intentions were peaceful. There was an even greater surprise. When she saw the chief of this Shoshone band, Sacagawea burst into tears of joy and threw her blanket over him as a gesture of love. He was her own brother, Cameahwait.

Lewis, Clark, York, and other members of the Corps are shown having a friendly encounter with Native Americans.

The Indians met with members of the Corps of Discovery in a tent set up by Captain Lewis. A translation chain was established. After Cameahwait spoke in Shoshone, Sacagawea translated his words into the Minnetaree language. Charbonneau then translated the words from Minnetaree into French. Finally, expedition member Francois Labiche translated what had been said from French into English for Lewis and Clark. Whenever the two captains spoke, the process was reversed.

Lewis and Clark made a deal with Cameahwait. They supplied the Shoshone with clothing, knives, and other goods in exchange for horses to help the expedition cross the Bitterroot Mountains.

Mist is rising in Big Creek Valley of the Bitterroot Mountains in Idaho.

CHAPTER FOUR

"Ocian in View! O! the Joy!"

The Corps of Discovery left the Shoshone tribe at the end of August, 1804. The explorers headed toward the Bitterroot Mountains, called by Patrick Gass the "most terrible mountains that I ever beheld."

The trip across the Bitterroot Mountains, which stand along the present-day Idaho-Montana border, was the hardest part of the journey. Falling snow soon reached the travelers' knees, causing people and the horses to stumble. Ill and weak from hunger, some of the travelers could barely walk. To survive, the explorers killed and ate a few of their horses. Finally, in late September, they completed the mountain crossing. On

In November 1805 the explorers passed through Cape Disappointment beach in Washington State.

September 22 Captain Lewis wrote in his journal about "the pleasure I felt in having triumphed over the mountains and descending once more to a level and fertile country."

The Corps of Discovery faced many more difficulties on their journey westward. Several times on the way to the Pacific Ocean, they met tribes of Indians. The Native Americans might have clashed with an all-male party of white men. But when they saw Sacagawea and her son, Pomp, they befriended and fed the explorers. Clark noted in his journal: "A woman with a party of men is a token of peace."

In October the expedition reached the Columbia River in what is now eastern Washington State. Rain pelted them day after day as they rowed down the Columbia on the last leg of their journey to the sea. The Columbia grew so wild that the voyagers became seasick. Giant logs nearly crushed their boats.

On November 7, 1805, came the moment the Corps of Discovery had eagerly awaited since they had first set out a year and a half earlier. They approached the Pacific Ocean. "We are in View of the Ocian, this great Pacific Octean which we have been So long anxious to See," wrote Clark. "Ocian in View! O! the joy!"

They had traveled more than 3,500 miles (5,633 km) to get there.

This replica of Fort Clatsop replaced the original fort, which rotted away by the mid–1800s.

CHAPTER FIVE

The Voyagers Return

The Corps of Discovery planned to spend the winter along the Pacific Coast before heading back east in the springtime. But where should they build their winter fort? A vote was held in which everyone—including Sacagawea and Clark's slave York—expressed their opinion. This was one of the rare occasions in early U.S. history that a woman or a slave was allowed to vote. The expedition members chose a spot near present-day Astoria, Oregon. There they built Fort Clatsop, named for the Clatsop Indians who lived nearby.

During the Corps of Discovery's three months at Fort Clatsop, it rained almost every day. The explorers passed the time by making

Lewis is shown shooting at an Indian. Except for this tragic event, all had been peaceful between the explorers and Native Americans.

moccasins to wear on the homeward journey. A bright spot of that dreary winter was Pomp's first birthday—February 11, 1806. Sacagawea's son was starting to walk and talk by then. Captain Clark had grown to love Pomp, whom he called "my little dancing boy."

The Corps of Discovery began their eastward journey on March 23, 1806. On the return trip, the explorers were again plagued by hunger and illness. Among the sick was Pomp, who suffered from a high fever and a swollen neck, due perhaps to the mumps or tonsillitis. The trip back through the mountains was once again very daunting. The travelers had to trudge through snow that was 15 feet (5 m) deep in places—in the month of June. During the following month, the most regrettable incident of the expedition occurred.

In July, Captain Lewis and three other men went off exploring in what is now Montana. They met several young Blackfoot Indians. The explorers and the Indians were **suspicious** of one another. A scuffle broke out over a gun. Reuben Field, one of the men with Lewis, stabbed a young Blackfoot to death. Lewis shot and killed another Blackfoot youth.

Two weeks later, Lewis himself was shot. On August 11, 1806, near what is now the Montana-North Dakota border, Captain Lewis and Pierre Cruzatte were out hunting. Lewis was aiming at an elk when he suddenly felt a severe pain near his hip.

"You have shot me!" he yelled.

Cruzatte, whose eyesight was poor, had evidently mistaken Lewis for an elk and shot him by accident in the thigh. Captain Lewis survived. But he developed a high fever from the wound and had trouble walking for some time.

A few days later the travelers returned to Fort Mandan. Lewis and Clark paid Charbonneau the $500 they had promised him, and they bid farewell to him, to Sacagawea, and to Pomp. The explorers then proceeded on to St. Louis. There, on September 23, 1806, they were greeted by cheering crowds. The expedition had traveled about 7,000 miles (11,265 km) since leaving the St. Louis area two years, four months, and nine days earlier. Having not heard from them for so long, many Americans had assumed that the explorers were dead.

During the 1800s settlers arrived in the Pacific Northwest to establish frontier towns.

"All the Success Which Could Have Been Expected"

Newspapers ran stories about the expedition's return. Meriwether Lewis, William Clark, and their men were welcomed as national heroes.

The Lewis and Clark Expedition paved the way for American settlement of the West. The explorers had visited what later became ten states. Seven of these states were made from lands bought from France as part of the Louisiana Purchase: Missouri, Kansas, Iowa, Nebraska, South Dakota, North Dakota, and Montana. The Corps of Discovery strengthened U.S. claims to the Pacific Northwest by also exploring what became Idaho, Washington, and Oregon. In their journals, Lewis and Clark and several of their men described and mapped places they had visited,

This map follows the Lewis and Clark Trail: The purple line traces the preparation, the green line, the recruitment, and the red line, the exploration.

which helped future westward travelers.

Among other things, the expedition discovered dozens of plants and animals that had been unknown to non-Indians. These included the pack rat, the Sitka spruce tree, and two birds named for the expedition's leaders, Lewis's woodpecker and Clark's nutcracker.

Unfortunately, later in the 1800s, white settlers heading west would push the Indians off their lands, sparking fights among Native American

HISTORY

OF

THE EXPEDITION

UNDER THE COMMAND OF

CAPTAINS LEWIS AND CLARK,

TO

THE SOURCES OF THE MISSOURI,

THENCE

ACROSS THE ROCKY MOUNTAINS

AND DOWN THE

RIVER COLUMBIA TO THE PACIFIC OCEAN.

PERFORMED DURING THE YEARS 1804—5—6.

By order of the

GOVERNMENT OF THE UNITED STATES.

PREPARED FOR THE PRESS

BY PAUL ALLEN, ESQUIRE.

IN TWO VOLUMES.

VOL. I.

PHILADELPHIA:

PUBLISHED BY BRADFORD AND INSKEEP; AND
ABM. H. INSREEP, NEWYORK.

J. Maxwell, Printer.

1814.

Lewis and Clark's journal and notes were first
published in 1814. This woodcut shows the title page.

tribes and whites. But except for the clash with the Blackfoot Indians, Lewis and Clark had, for the most part, established friendly relations with the Native American tribes they encountered.

In a message to Congress, the man who had ordered the expedition praised its accomplishments. The Corps of Discovery, said President Thomas Jefferson, had achieved "all the success which could have been expected." Lewis and Clark "and their brave companions," added the president, "have by this **arduous** service deserved well of their country."

Glossary

arduous—Difficult.

barge—Large, flat-bottomed boat designed to carry heavy loads in shallow water.

Corps of Discovery—The name for Lewis and Clark and the people who traveled with them. (A *corps* is a group of people organized for a specific purpose.)

Declaration of Independence—The paper, written by Thomas Jefferson in 1776, announcing the birth of the United States.

expedition—A long journey or trip.

Louisiana Purchase—828,000 square miles of land (2,144,000 square km) that the United States bought from France in 1803, now consisting of all or part of fifteen states.

moccasins—Soft footwear made of animal skins and originated by Native Americans.

pirogues—This often refers to a kind of canoe, but the pirogues used in the Lewis and Clark Expedition were large rowboats with sails.

portaging—The process of carrying boats or goods over land between two bodies of water or around obstacles such as waterfalls or rapids.

rapids—A portion of a river with fast-moving water.

sign language—Communication by means of hand gestures.

specimens—Samples that indicate what a group is like.

suspicious—Not trusting.

translate—To change words from one language into another.

Timeline

1607—Virginia, England's first permanent American colony, is established

1733—Georgia, England's thirteenth and final American colony, is established

1775—Americans begin fighting the Revolutionary War to free themselves from British rule

1776—On July 4 the Declaration of Independence, written by Thomas Jefferson, is approved

1783—By the Treaty of Paris, Britain recognizes the independence of the thirteen American colonies

1801—Thomas Jefferson, who is interested in westward expansion for the United States, becomes the nation's third president

1803—With the Louisiana Purchase, the United States acquires from France 828,000 square miles (2,144,000 square km) of land west of the Mississippi River

1607　　　*1783*　　*1803*

1804—The Lewis and Clark Expedition sets out from the St. Louis area to explore parts of the Louisiana Purchase and the Pacific Northwest

Winter 1804–05—The Corps of Discovery spends time at Fort Mandan, North Dakota, where Sacagawea joins them

November 1805—The Corps of Discovery arrives at the Pacific Ocean

Winter 1805–06—The Corps of Discovery spends time at Fort Clatsop, near present-day Astoria, Oregon

September 1806—The Lewis and Clark Expedition returns to St. Louis, completing a 7,000–mile (11,265–km) round-trip to the Pacific Coast

1906—The 100th anniversary of the completion of the Lewis and Clark Expedition

2006—The 200th anniversary of the completion of the Lewis and Clark Expedition

1804–06   *1906*   *2006*

Further Information

B O O K S

Alter, Judy. *Sacagawea: Native American Interpreter.* Chanhassen, MN: The Child's World, 2003.

Blumberg, Rhoda. *York's Adventures with Lewis and Clark.* New York: HarperCollins, 2004.

Bursell, Susan. *The Lewis and Clark Expedition.* Mankato, MN: Bridgestone Books, 2002.

Faber, Harold. *Lewis and Clark: From Ocean to Ocean.* New York: Marshall Cavendish, 2002.

Kimmel, Elizabeth Cody. *As Far As the Eye Can Reach: Lewis and Clark's Westward Quest.* New York: Random House, 2003.

Klingel, Cynthia, and Robert B. Noyed. *Lewis and Clark: Explorers.*
Chanhassen, MN: The Child's World, 2003.

Pringle, Laurence. *Dog of Discovery: A Newfoundland's Adventures with Lewis and Clark.* Honesdale, PA: Boyds Mills Press, 2002.

W E B   S I T E S

An excellent overview of the Lewis and Clark Expedition:
www.nps.gov/Jeff/LewisClark2/CorpsOfDiscovery/CorpsOfDiscoveryMain.htm

Home page for "Discovering Lewis & Clark," a Web site that describes
the expedition:
www.lewis-clark.org/

National Geographic Web site featuring a recreation of the Lewis
and Clark Expedition:
www.nationalgeographic.com/lewisandclark/

Bibliography

Ambrose, Stephen E. *Undaunted Courage: Meriwether Lewis, Thomas Jefferson, and the Opening of the American West*. New York: Simon & Schuster, 1996.

Chidsey, Donald Barr. *Lewis and Clark: The Great Adventure*. New York: Crown, 1970.

Coues, Elliott, editor. *The History of the Lewis and Clark Expedition by Meriwether Lewis and William Clark* (3 volumes). New York: Dover, 1987 (reprint of 1893 edition).

Holloway, David. *Lewis and Clark and the Crossing of North America*. New York: Saturday Review Press, 1974.

Schmidt, Thomas, and Jeremy Schmidt. *The Saga of Lewis and Clark: Into the Uncharted West*. New York: DK, 1999.

Index

Page numbers in **boldface** are illustrations.

maps
    Lewis and Clark Trail, 38
    Louisiana Purchase, 8

African Americans. *See* York

Cameahwait, 25–27
Charbonneau, Toussaint, 17–19,
    22, 26–27, 35
Clark, William, 10, **10**, 11, 18, **26**,
    34, 37–39
Corps of Discovery, 13

danger, 14, 22, 23–24, 29, 31, 34, 35
deaths, 14
dog, 11

food, 14, 16, 18, 21–22, 29
Fort Clatsop, 33–34
Fort Mandan, 14–19, **15**, **20**, 35

Jefferson, Thomas, 11, 21, 39
journals, 10, 13, 22, **23**, 31, 37–38,
    39

Lewis, Meriwether, 9, **9**, 11, **26**, **34**,
    35, 37–39
Louisiana Purchase, **6**, 7–11, **8**

mapping, 10, 38
mountains, **28**, 29, 34

Native Americans, 14–19, 21,
    24–27, **26**, 31, **34**, 35, 38–39

ocean, **30**, 31

Pacific Northwest, 11, **30**, **32**, **36**,
    37–39
plants and animals, 21, 23, 24, 25,
    38
Pomp, 18, 19, 21, 34, 39
public opinion, 35–37

return trip, 34–35
rivers, 13–14, 24, 25, 31

Sacagawea, 15–19, **17**, **18**, 21–27,
    31, 33, 35, 39
settlements. *See* Fort Clatsop; Fort
    Mandan
settlers, **36**, 37–38
slavery, 16, 33
    See also York
starting point, 13

team members, 11, 13, 14, 16, 19,
    27, 29, 35
territory covered, 14, 24, **25**, **28**,
    29–31, **30**, 35, 37, **38**
trade, 27
translation chain, 26–27, 31

transportation, **12**, 13–14, **15**,
    21–22, 27, 29, 34
    horses, 14–15, 18, 24–27, 29
    portage, 23–24

United States, **6**, 7, **8**, 22, **36**, 37–39

weather, 24, 29, 31, 33, 34
winters
    first, 14–19, **20**
    second, **32**, 33–34
women. *See* Sacagawea

York, 11, 16, **16**, **26**, 33

About the Authors

Dennis Fradin is the author of 150 books, some of them written with his wife, Judith Bloom Fradin. Their recent book for Clarion, *The Power of One: Daisy Bates and the Little Rock Nine*, was named a Golden Kite Honor Book. Another of Dennis's recent books is *Let It Begin Here! Lexington & Concord: First Battles of the American Revolution*, published by Walker. The Fradins are currently writing a biography of social worker and antiwar activist Jane Addams for Clarion and a nonfiction book about a slave escape for National Geographic Children's Books. Turning Points in U.S. History is Dennis Fradin's first series for Marshall Cavendish Benchmark. The Fradins have three grown children and three young grandchildren.